Black History Boy

Written
by
Michael D. Lambert

Illustrated by
Raymond P. Lambert III

Dedicated to our mother:

Sharion Gail Lambert

Let's Begin

There was a boy who loved black history.

He'd read book after book
learning all of it's mystery.

Egypt, Zimbabwe, Sudan and Timbuktu

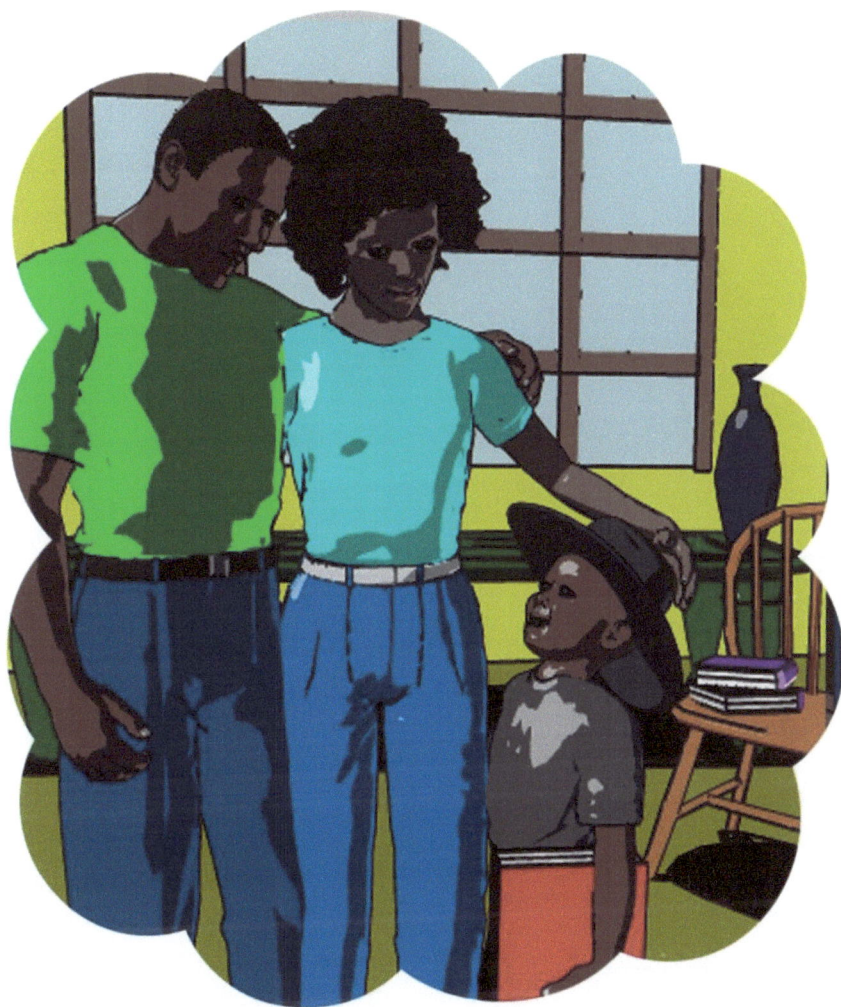

His parents joked, no one knew more than he knew.

The sounds of laughter,
outside children would play.

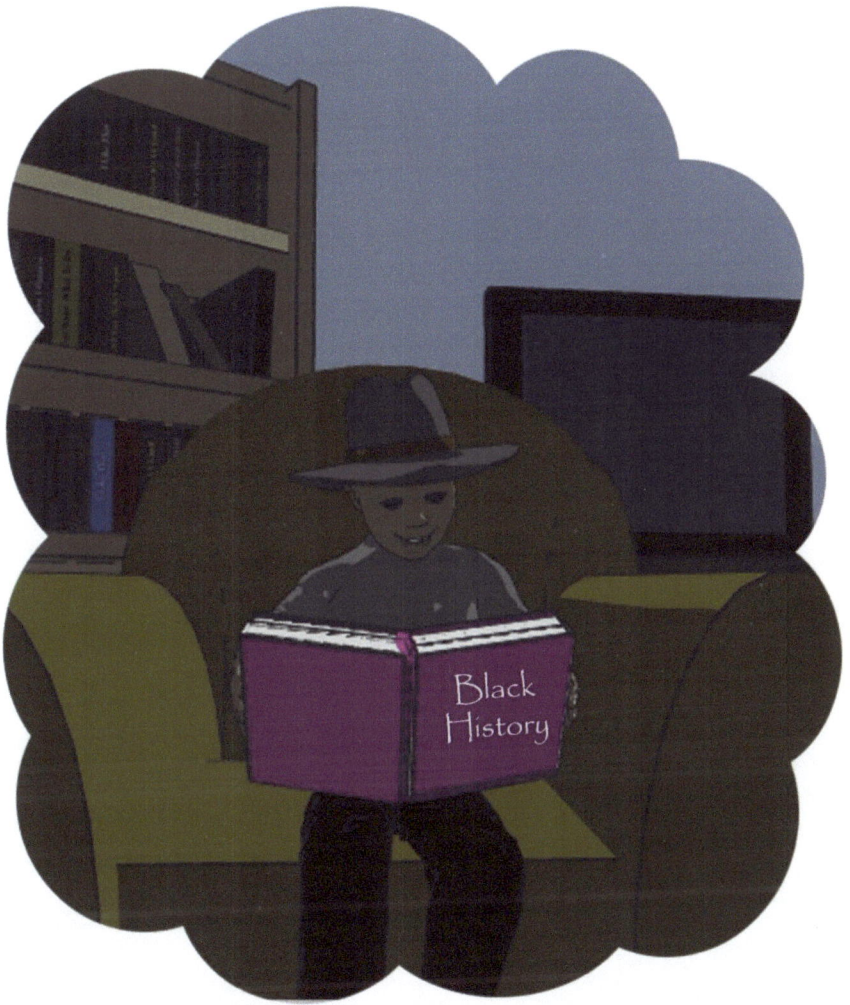

But in black history books,
buried his head would stay.

Niger, Rwanda, Kenya, Mozambique.

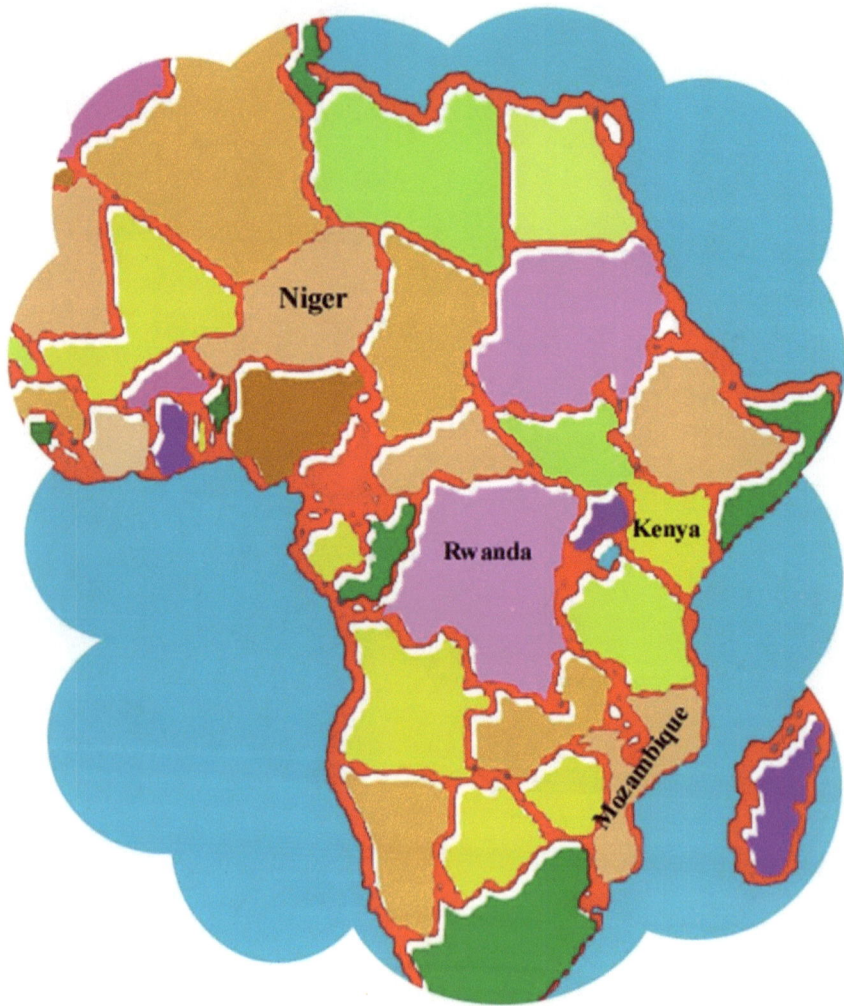

Library journies for knowledge
of these he'd seek.

Ashanti, Masai, Yoroba, and Zulu.

George Washington

Names never heard by him in school.

One day, he vowed, when he was a man...

He'd tell the story of Africa
the best that he can.

He'd say, people of earth,
it's where we all began.

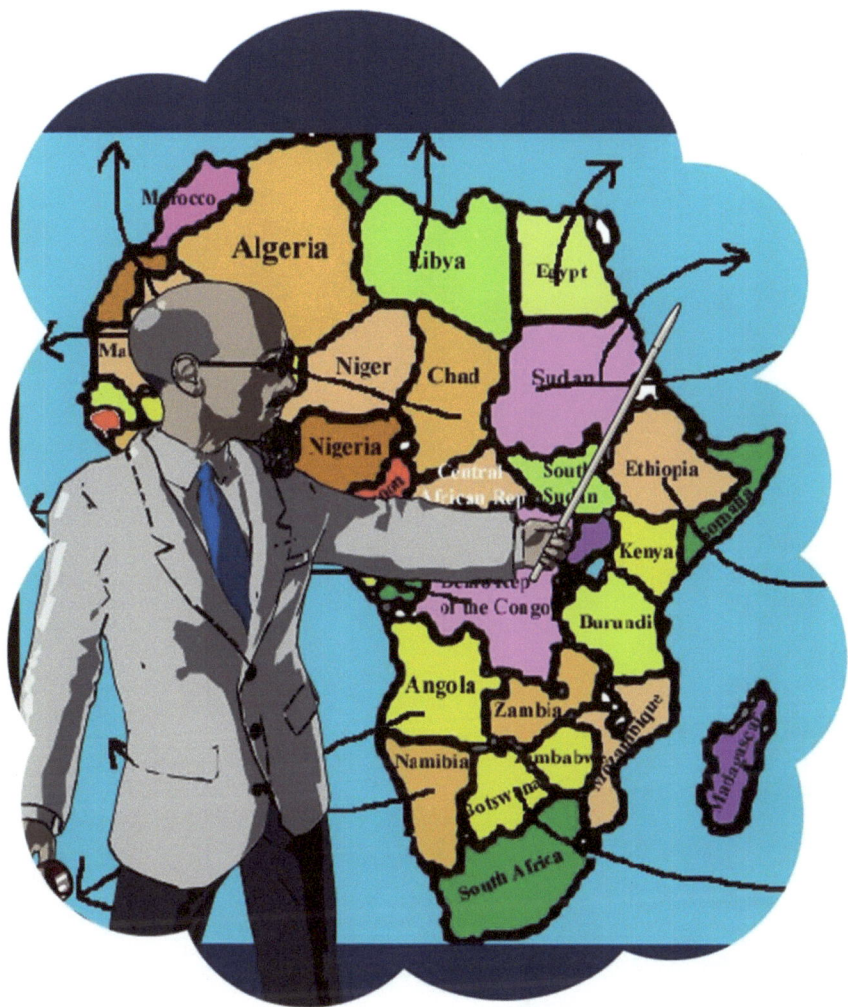

Scientist say it over and over again. . .

He would always say, if his dreams came true

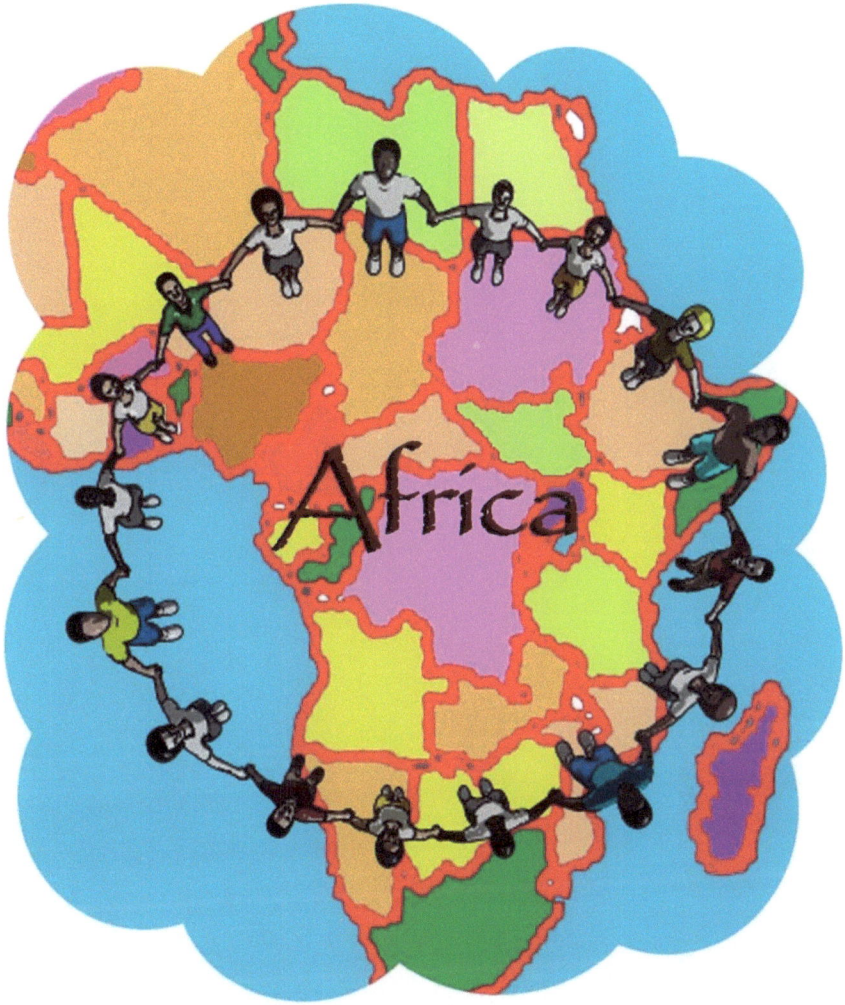

Everyone would love Africa
as much as I do.

Notes

Glossary I

Ashanti:
The Ashanti (or Asante), are the dominant ethnic group of a powerful 19th century empire and today one of Ghana's leading ethnic groups. They used female warriors in their army and in the Kings guard.

Egypt:
The Great Sphinx and the Pyramids of Giza were built during the Old Kingdom. A unified kingdom was founded 3150 BC by King Menes, leading to a series of dynasties.

Kenya:
The Great Rift Valley (in Kenya) is thought to be one of the places where human beings originated. Kenya's regions include swamps, mountains, deserts and forests. President Barack Obama's father was born in Kenya.

Masai:
The Maasai people live in southern Kenya and northern Tanzania along the Great Rift Valley. The Lion hunt is a historical practice that played an important role in the Maasai culture.

Glossary II

Mozambique:
The countries population of about 24 million is made up of mostly Bantu people. The largest religion in Mozambique is Christianity.

Niger:
For many centuries part of Niger was one of the most important provinces of the Kanuri Empire of Bornu. The might of Bornu was based on the control of a number of salt mines.

Rwanda:
Coffee is Rwanda's main export, accounting for 60% of the countries foreign exchange earnings. Tea accounts for about 30%.

Sudan:
What is now northern Sudan in ancient times was the kingdom of Nubia. Egypt and Nubia were ethnically and culturally similar.

Glossary III

Timbuktu:
Timbuktu started as a depot (near the Niger river) for commercial goods coming from the desert and grew into the learning center for which it became known. People came from all around to visit it's numerous libraries.

Yoruba:
Economically the Yoruba primarily engage in agriculture, with about 15% of the people employed as merchants or artists and craftsman.

Zimbabwe:
The name Zimbabwe means house of stone. The Shona who built the great Zimbabwe wall were ancestors of those who built Mapungubwe and Thulani in South Africa.

Zulu:
The word Zulu means "Sky".
In the early nineteenth century a young Zulu prince, Shaka, came onto the scene and combined most of the Nguni tribes into the powerful Zulu Nation.

ABOUT THE AUTHOR

The Author, Michael D. Lambert, also writes the award winning Black History web series (Black Archaeologist) where the lead character uses a time machine to visit great black peaple and civilizations of the past. Michael also produces the series with his brother Raymond P. Lambert III

www.ingramcontent.com/pod-product-compliance
Lightning Source LLC
Chambersburg PA
CBHW040145070426
42448CB00032B/43